Looking at . . . Deinonychus

A Dinosaur from the CRETACEOUS Period

For a free color catalog describing Gareth Stevens' list of high-quality books, call 1-800-542-2595 (USA) or 1-800-461-9120 (Canada). Gareth Stevens' Fax: (414) 225-0377.

Library of Congress Cataloging-in-Publication Data

Brown, Mike, 1947-
Looking at-- Deinonychus/written by Mike Brown; illustrated by Tony Gibbons.
p. cm. -- (The New dinosaur collection)
Includes index.
ISBN 0-8368-1140-2
1. Deinonychus--Juvenile literature. [1. Deinonychus. 2. Dinosaurs.] I. Gibbons, Tony, ill. II. Title. III. Series.
QE862.S3B765 1994
567.9'7--dc20 94-16969

This North American edition first published in 1994 by
Gareth Stevens Publishing
1555 North RiverCenter Drive, Suite 201
Milwaukee, Wisconsin 53212 USA

Consultant: Dr. David Norman, Director of the Sedgwick Museum of Geology, University of Cambridge, England.

Additional artwork by Clare Herronneau.

Printed in the United States of America

1 2 3 4 5 6 7 8 9 99 98 97 96 95 94

At this time, Gareth Stevens, Inc., does not use 100 percent recycled paper, although the paper used in our books does contain about 30 percent recycled fiber. This decision was made after a careful study of current recycling procedures revealed their dubious environmental benefits. We will continue to explore recycling options.

Looking at . . . Deinonychus

A Dinosaur from the CRETACEOUS Period

by Mike Brown

Illustrated by Tony Gibbons

Gareth Stevens Publishing
MILWAUKEE

Contents

Introducing Deinonychus

This book is about one of the most deadly dinosaurs of all – **Deinonychus** (DIE-NO-NIKE-US).

There were a lot of extraordinary things about **Deinonychus**.

It was not especially big for a dinosaur. In fact, it only stood a little bit taller than a fully grown human does today.

Most remarkable of all were the fearsome claws it had on its feet.

Join us on a safari back to Early Cretaceous times and the world of **Deinonychus**. But watch out! And take care not to make a sound! We are on the trail of a very clever and most ferocious beast.

Despite this, it was one of the fiercest creatures around, 110 million years ago, roaming what is now western North America.

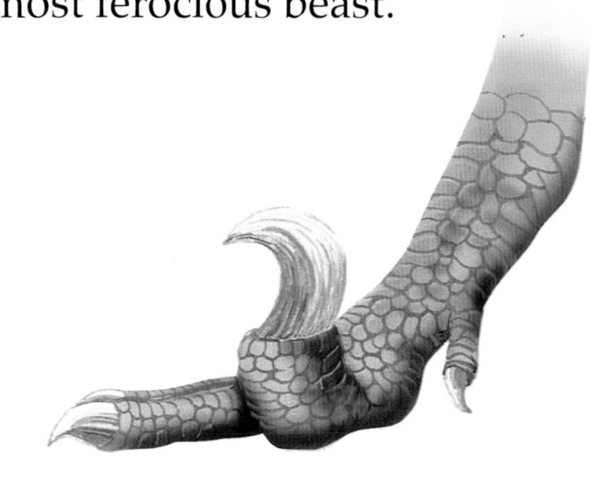

Terrible clawed creature

Deinonychus was, however, one of the most effective predators of all time.

Deinonychus was a meat-eater, hunting constantly for prey.

It was not very large, standing about 6.5 feet (2 m) tall and measuring about 10 feet (3 m) long. It weighed around 155 pounds (70 kg).

If humans had been around all those millions of years ago and had the misfortune to come face-to-face with a **Deinonychus**, they would probably have been able to recognize it right away. **Deinonychus** had a long, low head, and its jaws were filled with sharp, curving teeth – perfect for attacking prey.

Deinonychus's arms were long and muscular, with strong, grasping, three-fingered hands. Each finger had a claw that was used to grab victims.

Scientists think **Deinonychus** might have held its victim at a distance in order to kick at it with the claws on its feet. Its legs were powerful, and each foot had four toes – although the first, inner toe was tiny and backward-pointing and was not used very much. The other three toes were much larger, and each one had a hefty claw.

The largest claw was on the second toe. It was this weapon that gave **Deinonychus** its name, meaning "terrible claw."

Deinonychus's tail was probably held out straight behind for balance when it walked or ran. The tail was thick at the base and tapered toward the tip.

Small skeleton, fierce hunter

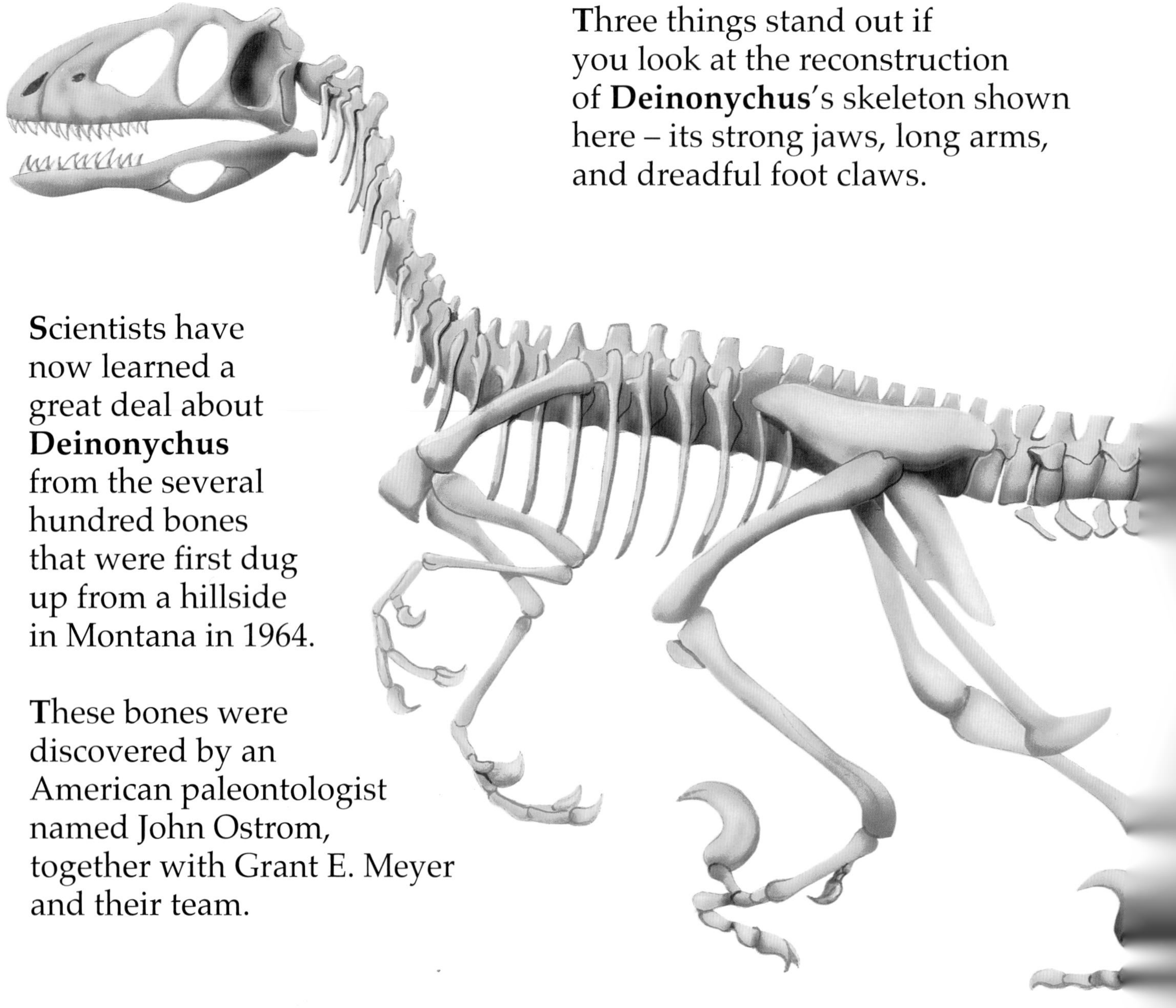

Three things stand out if you look at the reconstruction of **Deinonychus**'s skeleton shown here – its strong jaws, long arms, and dreadful foot claws.

Scientists have now learned a great deal about **Deinonychus** from the several hundred bones that were first dug up from a hillside in Montana in 1964.

These bones were discovered by an American paleontologist named John Ostrom, together with Grant E. Meyer and their team.

Deinonychus's skull was large and filled with holes (known as "windows") that made it lightweight. There were big openings for its eyes and plenty of space for the strong jaw muscles. These must have given **Deinonychus** a very powerful bite.

Look at how the teeth serrated and curved backward, helping **Deinonychus** tear meat from its victim. The more a victim struggled to get free, the more those teeth would bite!

Deinonychus could move its head around easily. Notice how the bones of its arms are almost as thick as its leg bones. This means its arms must have been quite powerful.

And just look at those clawed feet! These were this dinosaur's main weapon and were used to slash and kill as it held its prey at arm's length.

The last part of **Deinonychus**'s tail was stiffened with bony rods that enabled **Deinonychus** to hold its tail level when running. This helped the dinosaur maintain balance. One flick of the tail, and it could change its direction rapidly.

There are some skeletons of **Deinonychus** on display at the Museum of Comparative Zoology at Harvard University in Cambridge, Massachusetts.

This dinosaur's bones can also be seen at the Peabody Museum of Natural History at Yale University in New Haven, Connecticut. Some remains found in South Korea are also thought to be from a **Deinonychus**.

Predatory packs

When **Deinonychus**'s bones were first dug up, scientists found that they came from three **Deinonychus** skeletons lying close to each other.

Nearby, scientists also found the skeleton of a large plant-eater, **Tenontosaurus** (TEN-ON-TOE-SAW-RUS).

The three greedy **Deinonychus** must have been hunting in a pack and must have decided to attack the giant **Tenontosaurus** together.

This plant-eater was far bigger than a **Deinonychus** – so one **Deinonychus** could never have killed it alone. By working together, the three **Deinonychus** could have brought the larger animal down, leaping on it all at once and then tearing at it with their vicious claws.

If the **Tenontosaurus** had tried to run away, one **Deinonychus** might have grabbed the animal's tail and back legs to slow it down. The others, meanwhile, would probably have clung to its neck, chest, and belly, kicking with their clawed hind feet to wound and kill their huge prey.

Deinonychus may not always have hunted in a pack, however. It was a fast runner and could have chased other smaller dinosaurs on its own, such as the two-legged plant-eater **Hypsilophodon** (HIP-SEE-LOAF-OH-DON). It is also shown in this picture.

As soon as it had caught up with its prey, a single **Deinonychus** would have leapt onto the victim's back, dug its jaws into the animal's neck, and then, using the huge sickle claws on its feet, ripped the poor **Hypsilophodon** open.

Dreaded weapon

You should be glad that you were not around in **Deinonychus**'s time! Few animals were so well equipped for killing. It had powerful jaws for biting, sharp fangs for tearing at flesh, strong limbs for kicking, and heavy hand claws for grasping.

But it had one weapon that, above all others, made it truly terrifying. This was the sickle-shaped claw on the second toe of each foot.

These "terrible claws" grew to about 5 inches (13 centimeters) in length. They were not only huge but were also specially designed weapons used to slash victims. When **Deinonychus** walked along, it used its muscles to hold these huge claws off the ground to keep them sharp.

During an attack, **Deinonychus** would aim a deadly kick at a victim with a hind leg. The terrible claw would then flick forward with enormous force, slashing into the prey's flesh. A few kicks like this would have killed a poor victim, like the **Zephyrosaurus** (ZEF-EYE-ROE-SAW-RUS) shown here.

In Early Cretaceous times

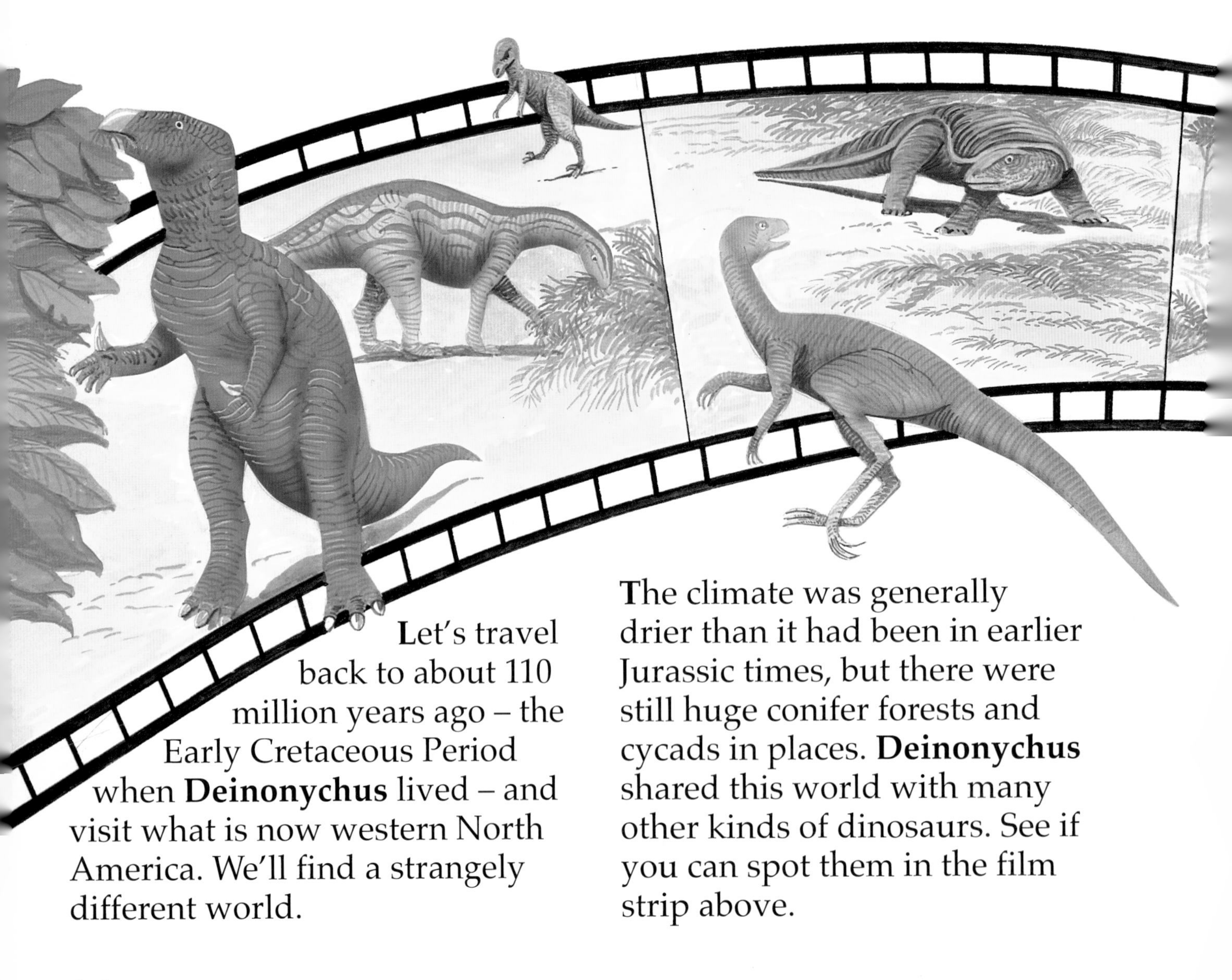

Let's travel back to about 110 million years ago – the Early Cretaceous Period when **Deinonychus** lived – and visit what is now western North America. We'll find a strangely different world.

The climate was generally drier than it had been in earlier Jurassic times, but there were still huge conifer forests and cycads in places. **Deinonychus** shared this world with many other kinds of dinosaurs. See if you can spot them in the film strip above.

Iguanodon (IG-WA-NO-DON), a plant-eater, or herbivore, was at least three times bigger than **Deinonychus** and had sharp thumb spikes for self-protection.

Trachodon (TRACK-OH-DON), another herbivore, had a toothless beak and a broad tail.

Deinonychus was the chief predator, but there was also **Microvenator** (MI-CROW-VEN-AT-OR), with a name meaning "tiny hunter." **Acrocanthosaurus** (AK-RO-KANTH-OH-SAW-RUS) was even longer than a bus!

Other plant-eaters included **Sauropelta** (SAW-RO-PEL-TA), a four-legged, armored creature about 23 feet (7 m) long, and **Hypsilophodon**. This little dinosaur was fast on its feet and had a horny, toothed beak, cheek pouches, and a stiff tail.

There were also other creatures around in Early Cretaceous times. There were winged reptiles called pterosaurs, primitive crocodiles, prehistoric turtles, and long sea creatures known as plesiosaurs.

The Archaeopteryx puzzle

Next time you feed the pigeons in a park, remember that you could be feeding a relative of the dinosaurs! At least, that is what some of today's scientists believe.

Birds, they say, may have evolved from such meat-eating dinosaurs as **Deinonychus**, although not everyone agrees.

A number of experts believe the earliest known bird was **Archaeopteryx** (AR-KEE-OP-TER-ICKS).

Its skeleton was first discovered in southern Germany in 1861. But **Archaeopteryx** was not very much like today's birds. It had small, pointed teeth and no beak, and a long, bony tail. In fact, it was more like a reptile in many ways – except that we know it had feathers. Prints of the feathers were found around the skeleton.

But it probably could not fly very well. Its wings were more like feathered arms, so it must have just fluttered in the air to catch insects. The feet, legs, and hips of **Archaeopteryx** were also very similar in structure to those of certain dinosaurs. So was it an early bird or a feathered dinosaur? Scientists are still trying to find out for sure.

Was Deinonychus

Many people used to think that dinosaurs were rather stupid animals with tiny brains. But, of course, no animal would survive for very long without intelligence. And we know dinosaurs roamed the Earth for 165 million years. That's far longer than human beings have existed!

Deinonychus was probably among the cleverest of dinosaurs. It had a relatively big brain – a help to a hunter because it had to be sharp enough to look for prey and catch it. This might have meant having to outwit another animal during the chase.

Deinonychus also needed a certain amount of skill to work together successfully.

intelligent?

Another clever dinosaur was **Troodon** (TROE-OH-DON) from the Late Cretaceous Period. It has often been called the brainiest of the dinosaurs because its brain was so large compared with the size of its body. **Troodon**, too, hunted in packs.

By comparison, **Stegosaurus** (STEG-OH-SAW-RUS) was not so bright. This large plant-eater, famous for the plates sticking up from its back, had a very small brain. In fact, it was not much bigger than a walnut!

But none of the the dinosaurs would have outshone you, if you could have sat together in a classroom!

Deinonychus data

The fiercest hunter of its time, **Deinonychus** was designed to attack prey, as several of its features show.

Backward-curved teeth

Deinonychus had masses of incredibly sharp teeth that had serrated edges, just like steak knives. These teeth also curved backward into the mouth. This meant that once **Deinonychus** had gripped prey in its jaws, the victim would have been unable to pull away, no matter how much it struggled to do so.

Sickle-shaped claws

Deinonychus's main weapon was the huge, sickle-shaped claw on the second toe of each foot. At 5 inches (13 cm) long, the claws were fearsome. Most of the time, they were held off the ground. But when **Deinonychus** needed them, the claws would be whipped forward to slash and tear at a victim. Few creatures would have survived such an attack!

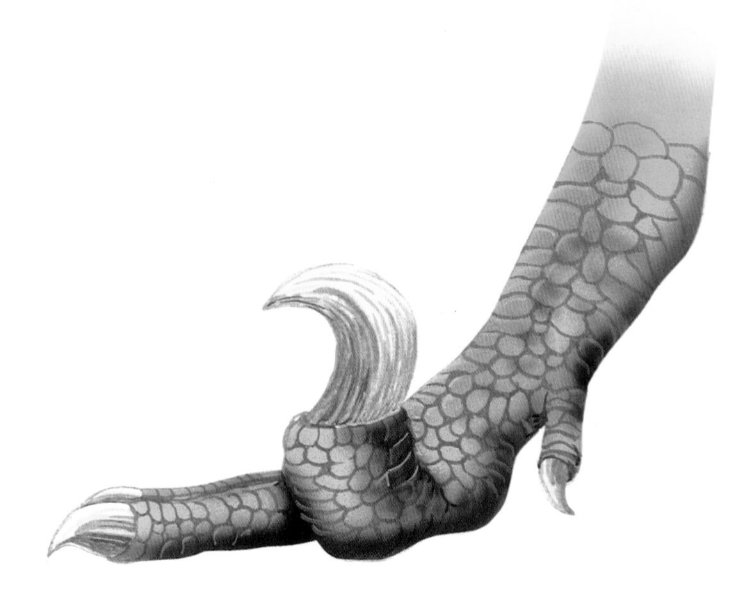

Bony tail

If you look back at pages 8-9 and examine **Deinonychus**'s skeleton near the hips, you will see that thin rods of bone surround the tail bones. These rods were attached to muscles that probably held the tail very stiff for balance when **Deinonychus** ran or stood on one leg to kick out with its deadly sickle claw. That's how the tail stayed as stiff and straight as shown here.

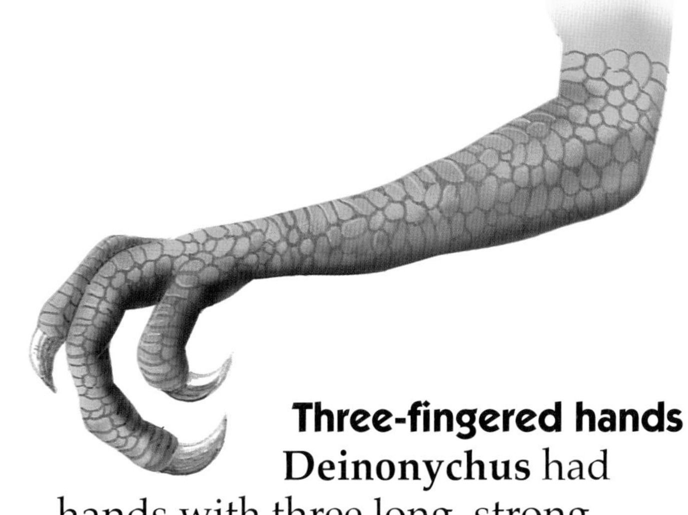

Three-fingered hands

Deinonychus had hands with three long, strong fingers. Each carried a mean-looking, sharply curved claw. Once the finger claws were dug into an animal, **Deinonychus** may then have been able to leap up and slash at the victim with its great sickle-clawed feet.

Long, powerful arms

The arms of some meat-eaters were quite small. Those of **Deinonychus**, however, were unusually long and muscular. It probably used them to hold its prey at arm's length so it would have space to kick out at the victim with its powerful, clawed feet.

So, if you want to spot a **Deinonychus** – or one of its close relatives – in an exhibition, film, or book, look for all of these features:

- sickle-shaped foot claws
- backward-pointing, sharp teeth
- a magnificent, stiff tail
- three strong, clawed fingers.

Deinonychus and relatives

Deinonychus (**1**) was the largest – and earliest – in a family of dinosaurs called the **Dromaeosauridae** (DROM-YEE-OH-SAW-RID-EYE), which means "running lizards." All these dinosaurs were two-legged meat-eaters. They were extremely fast and fierce, with sharp eyes and teeth and strong limbs.

Their most lethal weapons were the claws on their feet, which flicked forward when they attacked.

Dromaeosaurus (DROM-EYE-OH-SAW-RUS) (**2**) was only about half the length of **Deinonychus**.

When it stood up on its legs, though, **Dromaeosaurus** would have been tall enough to look you in the eye! It probably ate lizards, baby dinosaurs, and turtles. It lived in what is now Canada during the Late Cretaceous Period, about 80 million years ago.

Another relative was **Adasaurus** (AID-A-SAW-RUS) (**3**), which lived in Late Cretaceous Mongolia. This predator – its name means "demon lizard" – was about 6.5 feet (2 m) long, with a nasty toe claw, too.

About the same size as **Dromaeosaurus** was **Velociraptor** (VEL-AH-SI-RAP-TOR) (**4**). It, too, lived in Late Cretaceous times in Mongolia. Its name means "fast thief,"and it probably preyed on all sorts of small creatures. **Velociraptor** had long arms, slim legs, and sickle-shaped claws on its feet. The bones of one **Velociraptor**, dug up in 1971, showed that it had died in a fight with another dinosaur, **Protoceratops** (PRO-TOE-SER-A-TOPS). **Velociraptor** had been kicking it in the belly.

Saurornitholestes (SOAR-OR-NITH-OH-LESS-TEEZ) (**5**) lived in what is now Canada. It was about 6 feet (1.8 m) long and had hands with sharp claws. It, too, was a fast runner and had awesome foot claws.

1

2

Other dinosaurs had to beware when any member of this family was around, that's for sure!

GLOSSARY

conifers — woody shrubs or trees that bear their seeds in cones.

herbivores — plant-eating animals.

pack — a group of similar or related animals; a group of animals that travels or hunts together.

paleontologists — scientists who study the remains of plants and animals that lived millions of years ago.

pouch — a baglike part, such as that on a pelican's bill, used to carry and store food.

predators — animals that kill other animals for food.

prey — animals that are captured and killed for food by other animals.

remains — a skeleton, bones, or a dead body.

reptiles — cold-blooded animals that have hornlike or scale-covered skin.

skeleton — the bony framework of a body.

INDEX